IMAGES
of America

QUINCY

One of the earliest views of Quincy is seen in this rare carte d'visite, taken between 1859 and 1865. In the center is the courthouse and to the left is the Coburn House Hotel, which burned in December 1865. To the right of the courthouse and among the pine trees is the Masonic Hall, built in 1855.

IMAGES
of America

QUINCY

Scott J. Lawson
Plumas County Museum Association

ARCADIA
PUBLISHING

ISBN 978-1-5316-1489-8

Published by Arcadia Publishing
Charleston, South Carolina

Library of Congress Catalog Card Number: 2003109935

For all general information contact Arcadia Publishing at:
Telephone 843-853-2070
Fax 843-853-0044
E-mail sales@arcadiapublishing.com
For customer service and orders:
Toll-Free 1-888-313-2665

Visit us on the Internet at www.arcadiapublishing.com

The Plumas County Courthouse, built in 1859, is shown in this 1883 photograph. To its rear at left is the brick jail, and to the right behind the trees can be seen the Duncan Robertson home and the Dr. Stewart home (now Webster Engineering and Pete Hentschel Attorney at Law).

CONTENTS

ACKNOWLEDGMENTS

Lois Alexander, Marjorie Lee Clark, Jim Gossett, Don Johns, Scott Kelly, Dean Lawson, Ernest Leonhardt, Ruth Reid, and Zola Stokes. Also a posthumous thank you for their dedication in collecting and identifying photographs goes to Mary Phelps Dunn, Edna Cole Gifford, Helen Hall Lawry, and Violet Cole Mori.

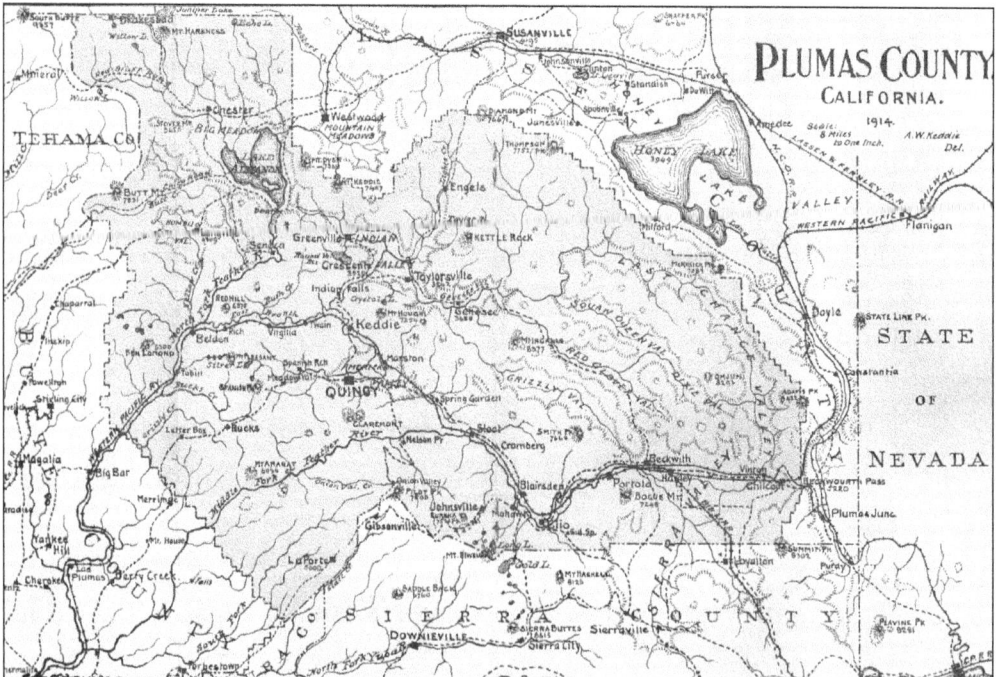

This 1914 map shows Plumas County, located in northeastern California, with centrally located Quincy, the county seat.

INTRODUCTION

Quincy, California, is a picturesque community of some 5,500 people nestled into the south side of the American Valley in central Plumas County. Surrounded by timber-clad hillsides and snow-capped peaks, its nickname, "The Gem of the Sierras," is a fitting description.

In June of 1850 the Turner brothers claimed all the land south of Spanish Creek that now encompasses Quincy. They supported, in spirit, if not in cash, mountain man Jim Beckwourth's efforts to bring an emigrant wagon trail through the valley on its way from the Nevada desert to the Sacramento Valley. Even without their financial support Beckwourth's Trail did result in some parties staying and establishing homes in the American Valley. Among them were Lewis Stark and others who were instrumental in discovering the rich gold placers at Elizabethtown in the fall of 1852. Hugh J. Bradley purchased land from the Turners in the summer of 1852 and established a stopping place called the American Ranch, by which name the small community became known for a time. Farmers began taking up ranches, and soon, the first sawmill, gristmill, and blacksmith shop were established in the valley.

Although the small community of American Ranch was already established, it is generally accepted that Quincy proper made its debut with the birth of the county in 1854. On March 18, 1854, an act was passed by the State of California creating Plumas County from the eastern portion of Butte County. John Thompson, Wilson Seaman Dean, and Hugh J. Bradley were appointed commissioners to set up the elections for county officers and a county seat. At this point, the spirited gold camp of Elizabethtown developed the notion it should become the county seat. However, its canyon-like location was inferior to that of the more expansive American Valley. Bradley's offer to donate land for a courthouse in exchange for the county seat and the name of Quincy, after his hometown in Illinois, was accepted by the county's voters. American Ranch was renamed Quincy and designated the county seat.

Of course all of this ignored the original inhabitants of the American Valley, the Maidu Indians, who had lived in the valley for centuries before the white man came. Forced from their ancestral homes along the valley's southern exposure by agricultural development, many attached themselves to the new ranches and became domestic servants and ranch hands.

Until recently, emigration to Quincy was based on mostly economic factors. As Plumas County's gold mines prospered, many miners, including great numbers of Chinese moved into the area. Since then, the Chinese have largely disappeared; when the gold gave out most went elsewhere. A few remained, but for the most part, all that is left is a Chinese cemetery, place names, and the remains of the roads, ditches, and other projects they helped build. Roads and communication lines developed; first telegraph, then the telephone, linked Quincy to the outside world. During the 1870s the area was in full economic boom as the gold poured from the hydraulic mines. Come the turn of the century, for various reasons gold mining was starting to decline and the timber industry was beginning an upward swing. In 1910, the newly completed

Western Pacific Railroad connected Quincy with the rest of the world economically. With gold and copper mining still a viable revenue source, the timber industry's rapidly increasing development, and agriculture's steady output, turn-of-the-20th-century Quincy looked better than it ever had economically. A sawmill sprang up where today's Plumas Pines Shopping Center is located. During the late 1930s and into the 1950s, mill owner C.A. King brought a large number of African Americans from Lake Charles, Louisiana, to Quincy to work in the mill. Although the mill closed many years ago, many of King's employees remained, raising their families, attending local schools, and becoming a part of the community.

Quincy's Main Street, laid out in an east-west fashion, developed a business section that clustered near the county square. A collection of log and other rustic buildings first sprang up, but with the new courthouse and community pride, more handsome buildings replaced the early structures. These too were modified as time marched along; fires took their toll, new owners wanted a new look, more substantial structures were erected, but for the most part the business section maintained its original flavor. A catastrophic fire in August 1934 leveled many of the original wooden business structures, but a few of the early buildings still remain to this day, recognizable, though there are some changes from their original appearance. In 1919 a new courthouse was built to replace the 1859 structure that had served the county for over 60 years. In 1937 the Feather River Highway was completed, allowing easier auto travel to and from the county seat.

Since Quincy's inception, three hotels have come and gone on the site of the new Dame Shirley Plaza; numerous buildings on Main Street have been replaced by fire, economics, and time, and scores of attractive homes built, particularly along historic Jackson Street. Growth has occurred in all directions, but particularly in East Quincy, once a few ranches, some residences, and several businesses, such as the Stone House and Boyd's Market. During the 1950s, a business strip development along Highway 70 East took place, and south of it, housing developments, notably Amervale, were built. Since then, scores of new businesses, the county fairgrounds, a new high school, new grammar schools, and a community college have been built. Long touted as one of the only counties in the state left without a stoplight, that also changed about ten years ago. For all its existence, Quincy's economy has relied on natural resources, particularly the timber industry. Due to various factors, a large reduction in that sector has seen a greater dependence on the tourism industry. Visitors now come to enjoy the county's outdoor recreation opportunities, as well as Quincy's cultural and historical amenities.

Today, a small group of dedicated people that love Quincy's history still endeavors to protect Quincy's historic areas for the enjoyment, and edification not only of today's residents, but also for those generations of residents and visitors to come.

In this c. 1900 photograph, the Methodist Church, built in 1876, is seen before the front porch was added. To its right is the parsonage, moved from Main Street in 1881. Next is the George Wilson Home, built in 1895; its foundation is made of rocks salvaged from Elizabethtown's ruins.

One

AMERICAN VALLEY'S FIRST INHABITANTS AND EARLY SETTLERS

Quincy in 1860.

This is the earliest known dated photograph of Quincy, taken in 1860. It shows the county courthouse right of center. To its left and partially behind a tree is the three-story Coburn House Hotel, and just past the courthouse are the Harbison House (pictured on the cover) and the American Ranch Hotel.

This approximately 1880s view shows the American Valley with hydraulic mining debris-choked Spanish Creek at left. The mines on upper Spanish Creek sent down so much debris that at one point they caused flooding and damage to property along Lawrence Street. A canal was cut through the valley in the late 1870s to channel the debris away from town. This view shows the canal pretty well filled.

The Maidu Indians lived for centuries along the foot of the hills on the valley's edges. When the white people invaded their homeland during the gold rush, they were displaced onto ranches and on the edge of towns. Mary Hamilton is shown holding her granddaughter with daughter Bessie, while her husband, John Hamilton, is at right. They are shown near their home three miles north of Quincy.

(*right*) John Wesley Thompson was one of American Valley's earliest settlers. First owning a business at the mining camp of Nelson Point in 1850, he later moved to a ranch on the La Porte Road, which remained in his family until about 1915. Thompson was also one of the three commissioners appointed to conduct the formation of Plumas County in 1854. He died in 1905.

(*below*) James Edwards and his wife, Jane (at right), came to American Valley in 1855, built the Plumas House hotel in 1866, and operated it for many years. When James passed away in 1882, his son Will assumed management of the business.

(*left*) Wilson Seaman Dean, pictured here in the 1860s, came to Quincy in 1851. He ran a store in Meadow Valley and was the first man to drive a stage over the Oroville-Quincy Road. Dean was also one of the three commissioners appointed to form Plumas County. He was also tax collector and sheriff and lived in Quincy with his wife, Sarah. Dean died in 1918 at age 87.

(*below, left*) William E. Ward came to Quincy with his parents in 1853 at age 11. He apprenticed in the newspaper business, and in 1869 purchased the *Plumas National*, which he ran for a number of years. Ward later left to sojourn around the western United States before passing away in 1930 at age 87.

(*below, right*) Dr. John S. Vaughn is pictured here in 1864. Vaughn came to Plumas County in the early 1850s and practiced at Nelson Point, then Quincy. He was noted for his drinking binges and carousing ways.

(*right*) Arthur W. Keddie came to Plumas County from Canada in 1864 as a land surveyor. One of his first important tasks was to survey a wagon road through the Feather River Canyon. Instead he recognized the canyon's potential as a railroad route and for the next 40 years promoted his idea. It finally came to fruition with the completion of the Western Pacific Railroad in 1909. Keddie is shown here on May 18, 1865.

(*below, left*) Kentucky native James Humphrey Haun was an early Quincy resident, having come here in 1853 to mine gold. After a stint on nearby Nelson Creek he bought the American Ranch where he and his wife farmed and raised a large family. James and his son John kept extensive diaries of their experiences here.

(*below, right*) Martha Hurst Haun, also a Kentuckian, arrived in Quincy via hand sled over the snows from La Porte in 1855. She joined her husband, James, and son John at the American Ranch where, besides farming, they took in travelers.

Peter Mason Day came to Plumas County in 1852 by way of Beckwourth Pass and was one of the original settlers at Elizabethtown. After the gold diggings petered out he moved his family to Quincy where he was a teamster. Day died in 1911 at age 79.

Lewis Stark brought a wagon train of emigrants over Beckwourth Pass in 1852. They discovered gold north of Quincy and established Elizabethtown. The first justice of the peace and postmaster for American Valley, Stark later moved to Indian Valley where he died in 1891.

William W. Kellogg came to Plumas County in 1858 and remained until his death at age 95 in 1933. He was elected county assessor, clerk, school trustee, state assemblyman, and state senator, and in later years was a respected local historian. A lawyer, he also owned the Quincy Union and the La Porte Union newspapers during the 1860s. This photograph was taken c. 1915.

Nancy Reid Yeates and James Hughes Yeates are shown here holding their grandchildren at the Huskinson Home in Quincy around 1900. The Yeates came to Plumas County in 1851 over Beckwourth Pass and, after acquiring a ranch in 1862, lived on it for the rest of their lives. They raised a family of eight children. James Yeates served as county sheriff for four terms.

Warren A. Blakesley was one of Elizabethtown's first residents and married Elizabeth Stark for whom the town was named. Blakesley, a freight teamster, died in 1902.

Elizabeth Stark Blakesley is shown here much later in life than when she was honored by the naming of Elizabethtown. "Betsyburg" and "Sister Betsy's Gulch" were other names given to the town that lasted from 1852 until about 1865. Elizabeth died in 1918.

Two

QUINCY'S COMMERCIAL ESTABLISHMENTS

At the time this photograph was taken of Quincy around 1895, there was an open area left from the fire that consumed the Quincy Hotel and several businesses. The structures, from left to right, are Stephan's Livery Stable, Asher Cohn's brick store, Colonel Wyatt's Bank Building, the Capitol Saloon, a meat market, Kaulback's Dry Goods, Quincy Drug Store, and the town hall.

The north side of Quincy's Main Street is pictured about 1877 in a celebration by the International Order of Odd Fellows. The two brick structures on the left were completed in September of 1876, while the Capitol Saloon in the center was built in 1873. The white building was a dry goods store that burned around 1890.

This view of a dismal winter day in 1884 looks north at the Dew-Drop-Inn, to its left the Fletcher-Muller Building, and left of that the stove and tin shop that was later to become Feather Publishing. These buildings sat on the site now occupied by the Plumas County Permit Center.

This view of Quincy's Main Street looks west about 1895. At the left edge are the 1850s Harbison House, an unidentified house, Lee's Store, and the Plumas House Hotel at the end. On the right is a wagon hoist for Light's blacksmith shop, four unidentified buildings, the town hall, Quincy Drug, Dorsch's Hardware, a meat market, the Capitol Saloon, the Wyatt Building, and Cohn's Store.

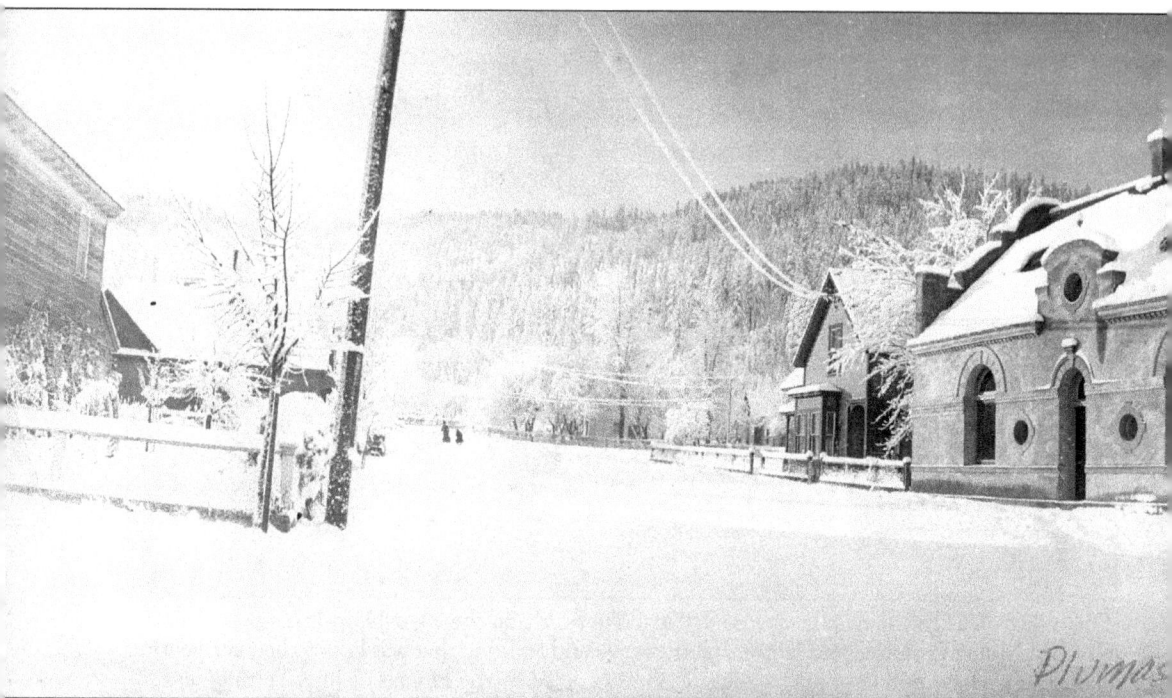

This c. 1905 view of Main Street looking southwest centers on the 1903 Plumas County Bank. Note that the door on the side is now a window. Behind the bank is the J.F. Spooner residence;

This early spring 1906 shot of Crescent and Main streets presents a sleepy appearance. At left is

Fire Hall   Plumas House

to the right of the bank is the open lot now housing the rock-faced Clinch Building, then the fire hall, Lee's Store, and at the end of the street, the Plumas House.

the Plumas House; in the center is the Plumas House Livery Stable, then the business section.

The *Plumas National*, the longest running newspaper in Quincy, had moved from its original spot on Main Street to this Harbison Street location. On February 21, 1890, the snow measured at 7.5 feet.

A name change and a change of location occurred in 1892 when the *Plumas National* and the *Greenville Bulletin* combined to form the *Plumas National-Bulletin*. In 1932 the paper's name was changed to the *Feather River Bulletin*. In 1978 a three-story brick building supplanted all the earlier structures. On the extreme left is Watt Bell, and on the right is editor Felix Grundy Hail.

The *Plumas Independent* was established in 1892 by A.A. Hall in this 1860s restaurant. From left to right are George Porter Hall, unidentified, Andrew "Doc" Hall, son Arthur Hall, and Hugh Porter. The county demolished the building in 1973 with the widening of Grover Alley.

This 1890s interior view of the *Plumas Independent* shows, from left to right, Arthur A. Hall, an unidentified man and boy, Watt Bell, and George Porter Hall. This newspaper ran until 1945 at which time the *Feather River Bulletin* printing interests acquired it.

This 1903 photograph shows the Plumas County Bank and its directors and employees posed in front. Note the entrance on the left side that is now a window. From left to right are Clark J. Lee, Will Clinch, Harley Flournoy, Judge John D. Goodwin, Cy Tregaskis, Ted Huskinson, and Harry Lee.

Quincy Drug Store presented a spic-n-span appearance in 1900 when owners Abbie and Barney Schneider posed for this photograph.

24

S.L. Bailey, who had acquired the Quincy Drug Store in 1932, is shown weighing placer gold on his apothecary scales. Bailey bought over $10,000 worth of gold a year from the Depression-era miners. Bailey's partner Barrett Huskinson sold his interest to O. Van Gilder, who, along with Bailey, ran the business until Bailey's son Barry and wife Peggy purchased it. Jim and Joanie Ellingson purchased the store from the Baileys on October 1, 1989, and sold it to Mike and Karen Kibble, the present owners, on October 31, 2003.

The Rexall Drug Store offered competition as well as appliances. Shown here in the 1950s are Freeman "Bud" Grover (left) and Alan McClard featuring a new Sunbeam electric saucepan.

The Quincy Hotel was built after the Coburn House Hotel burned in 1865. This large hotel sat on the site of present-day Ayoob's clothing store on Main Street until about 1890 when a fire consumed it also.

The Grand Central Hotel was built c. 1897 on the site of the earlier Quincy Hotel and what is today Ayoob's clothing store and remained there until fire erupted from its rear on August 28, 1934. For years the Grand Central was a favorite along with the Plumas House and Hotel Quincy.

The first Plumas House Hotel, a log building, was built by Billy Houck, George W. Sharpe, and E.H. Pierce around 1853. It burned in 1863 and James Edwards erected a frame building in 1866. This *c.* 1870 view was taken from the courthouse yard. The Plumas House was known far and wide as the "finest hotel in the mountains" for over half a century.

This *c.* 1875 shot of the Plumas House shows the addition of a bay window on the south end as well as an addition to the two-story section at the rear of the building. Note the trees in front and along the side.

The morning of July 5, 1880, found the Gibsonville Band loading onto stages at the Plumas House for the trip home over the La Porte Road. They had come to Quincy to play at the Fourth of July celebration. By this time there were dormers added to the third story, and a few years later a two-story annex was added to the south end of the hotel.

In this photograph, taken about 1907, is a group of autos on a trip through Quincy. From left to right the cars are a 1905 Packard Model 30 Touring Car, a Locomobile, and two 1907 Oldsmobile Touring Cars. The rest are unidentified but also look like Oldsmobiles. Still a profitable business, the magnificent Plumas House fell to fire on June 3, 1923.

This 1890 interior view of the Plumas House shows, from left to right, Charles Rupert, W.J. Miller, John McQuin, and an unidentified man. Behind the bar are owner W.J. Edwards and William Beyers.

After the Plumas House burned in June 1923, construction of a new hotel was undertaken and completed on October 31, 1925. In this early autumn 1925 photograph note the wagon in Court Street and the finishing touches being applied to the new building.

WINTER NITE
QUINCY CALIF.

The Hotel Quincy was the civic center of Quincy for many years, hosting activities of clubs such as Rotary, the 20-30 Club, and the chamber of commerce. There were 24 rooms and excellent kitchen and dining facilities, as well as a bar called the Happy Hollow, but known as the Sump (because of its subterranean location). This *c.* 1950 night scene shows the hotel in winter finery.

The Hotel Quincy stood as a landmark for the next 41 years until it too succumbed to fire like its predecessors. In the early hours of November 27, 1966, a fire leveled the historic structure. Recently, the lot was acquired by the county and renovated into Dame Shirley Plaza for use by the public.

This 1890s interior view of the Capitol Saloon shows the upstairs card and billiard room. The man at right is owner Ed Huskinson.

The Capitol Saloon has been housed in the same brick building since 1873. In later years the back bar was moved from its original location on the east wall to the west wall. Identified in this 1910 photograph are Jack Knight, Tom Larimore, and Clarence Moseley, but in no particular order.

The 1859 Buckhorn Brewery was a large, rambling building at the corner of High Street when this *c.* 1900 photograph was taken. From left to right are Johann Conrad Eddlebuttle, J.C. Werner, John P. Dietman (Dutch John), and Charles Stiffen. A small private zoo was kept there also.

Looking inside the Buckhorn Brewery & Saloon one understands how it came by its name. The walls are adorned with antlers behind the bar where Chris Werner presides. First William Schlatter, then the Werners, made their locally famous beer here with water diverted from Boyle Ravine to a holding tank. The building was razed in 1940.

This interior view of the butcher shop in the Clinch Building shows, from left to right, William Clinch, an unidentified man, and Henry Orr, the butcher. Note the lath and plaster still under construction on the wall.

The Plumas Club was originally called Harvey's Place for its owner Harvey Egbert, who built it about 1914. During Prohibition, Ed Dory ran it as the Quincy Dairy Store. Along with sodas and shakes, there were slot machines and a restaurant added a little later. Ed is shown behind the counter in this 1933 photograph. The tin ceiling and back bar are there to this day.

McIntosh's Hardware had practically everything anyone could want. Surrounded by tin ware, tools, crockery, and dry goods are, from left to right, Morgan Haun, Arch Braden, Ed. C. Kelsey, and Melvin McIntosh. This store burned in the 1934 fire.

Fresh vegetables, canned fruits, crackers, noodles, flour, coffee, tea, and more dress up the shelves of J.C. Cloman's Red & White Grocery on the north side of Main Street. This building was built about 1915 and was the east end of the 1934 fire. In this 1923 photograph is Jim Cloman at left and on the right is Harry Glendenin.

This interior view of C.J. Lee's Store on Main Street shows, from left to right, Mary Elizabeth Miller Lee, John Corydon Lee, Mildred Elizabeth Lee, and Clark Joshua Lee. The last two men are unidentified. This is now the Pizza Factory.

This exterior view of Lee's Store was taken about 1920. Abe Bar (center) bought the store from Clark Lee in 1916 and remodeled its exterior. At left is Lewis Bar, Abe's son; at right is George I. Chaffey, a carpenter who added the extension to the 1905 Quincy school.

W.F. Stone (left) rented a shop from Harry Muller (right) for his watch repairing business, situated where the Plumas County Permit Center now stands. The locust tree at right still stands along the street today, though the building was razed in the 1940s.

In this 1910 view, watchmaker John W. Street poses with attorney H.B. Wolfe in front of their businesses on Main Street. This ornate building, known as the Steel Front Building, is opposite the courthouse and housed Bob's Café for many years. To the left of the men are the arched windows and entrance to the Capitol Saloon.

This May 1934 view looking east on Main Street is one of the last pictures of the old wood buildings before the fire that would occur in August of that same year. Despite the fire, the street lamps on the power poles would survive at least through the late 1950s.

The afternoon of August 28, 1934, saw the eruption of a fire in the laundry behind the Grand Central Hotel. Although firefighters were throwing water on it immediately, the wooden structure was consumed in a very short time, and the fire quickly spread east on the north side of Main Street.

Tom Ayoob (left) and Olga Ayoob carry boxes of merchandise rescued from their burned store to the safety of the courthouse lawn.

This view from the courthouse lawn shows merchandise saved from the fire that, at the time of this shot, is consuming the hardware store, Quincy Drug, and the town hall.

The Grand Central Hotel is completely leveled in this photograph. The building at left, known as the Steel Front Building, was built about 1895, and was, until the fire, the most ornate business structure in Quincy. It was completely refaced after the fire and housed Bob's Café and other businesses for many years.

Like a scene from a war, the fire of August 28, 1934, claims its last two victims, Quincy Drug and the town hall.

The ruins of the town hall lean against the west wall of the Red & White Grocery in this August 29, 1934 shot of the devastation of the fire of the previous day. In all, 7 buildings were completely destroyed and 18 businesses were burned out. Several other buildings survived with severe damage.

This group of masonry buildings on Main Street survived the fire of August 1934, though soot remains on the side of J.C. Cloman's Red & White Grocery. This 1935 view looks to the east.

Reconstruction and repairs after the fire are underway in this 1935 photograph of Main Street. Missing from the picture is the Bank Club building on the corner of Bradley and Main. It would come along the next year.

Quincy's Main Street during the 1950s presents a somewhat cluttered appearance. The view looks to the east.

This late 1950s view of Main Street shows some changes from the preceding photograph. Note the transformation of the Plumas Garage into Western Auto, as well as the makeover of the hardware store next door. The Hotel Quincy "Koffee" Shop sign also makes its debut.

The early 1950s presented this view of Quincy when entering from the north. On the right is Skillern Chevrolet, then the car lot entrance to Quincy Motor Sales, an old residence, Cotter's Chrysler dealership and Flying "A" gas station, and of course, the Plumas County Courthouse.

This eastward view up Lawrence Street was taken by the sheriff's office but for unknown reasons. On the right is the Union 76 gas station, then Moseley & Grenke's Market.

Paul Sprague built the Log Cabin Theater in the 1930s on a lot now occupied by the back end of the Quincy Post Office. It burned in the mid-1950s and, after standing vacant for a time, was razed. In 1963 Safeway opened their new building on the site of the Log Cabin Theater, then moved to Plumas Pines Shopping Center in 1976.

Jessie and Joe Crivello stand proudly in front of their newly opened Hi Spot Drive In, located across the road from the Quincy High School. Later known as "Fred's," this and nearby Carl's Drive In provided 19¢ burgers to a generation of high school students.

This late 1975 view looking west shows Quincy's Main Street being excavated for the one-way traffic project that would route traffic east on Main Street and west on Lawrence Street.

Three

INDUSTRY AND TRANSPORTATION

Woodcutting is still hard work even with today's chainsaws, wood splitters, and pickup trucks. In 1886 hand saws, mauls, and wedges were the only way for Charles G. Heath, Nathan McDonald, and Thomas O'Haviland to cut literally hundreds of cords of wood. It is not certain if O'Haviland has the gun to keep the men working or if it is to protect their investment.

This is thought to be John Ritchie at the Thompson or Illinois Ranch sharpening his scythe. During the early years of farming, this was the only method for cutting hay.

Agriculture always played a large role in American Valley's economy. Shown here is the Mill's Ranch haying crew *c.* 1900. From left to right are (front row) Arthur Bonny, unidentified, Solon Jacks, and John Brinkers; (back row) unidentified, Esler Jones, Ira Wixom, Will E. Mills (manager), Ed Lucas, unidentified, Bob Hedrick (Maidu), and unidentified.

The Mill's Ranch, now Feather River College, sported state-of-the-art animal husbandry in 1900. The cattle were housed in an elevated section so that the manure would drop below. Those pictured are, from left to right, F. Luman, S. Bull, C. Grover (on ramp), Coodles (dog), and R. Remick.

Quincy was the hub of commerce for the area's mines and mills. Shown here in 1903 is Asher B. White and his daughter Charlotte at the Bean Hill Mine about eight miles west of Quincy. Quincy Mining & Water Company and others like it were a welcome part of the economy of Quincy.

Quincy's townspeople turned out to watch as track was laid on the Western Pacific north of Quincy near Quincy Junction in 1909. By November, the last spike would be driven at the Keddie trestle about five miles distant, connecting American Valley to the rest of the world.

R.D. "Tune" Haun is shown driving Gansner's ox team with a two-log load in 1897. The logs are headed west through Quincy to the Gansner Mill, one mile distant. Until the advent of the railroad in 1910, most lumbering was for local consumption. After 1910, local lumber was shipped to worldwide markets.

The Quincy Lumber Company commenced operations in the fall of 1913 when they constructed a three-quarter-mile-long log chute southeast up Hangman's Ravine and began logging the hillside opposite the cemetery. In this view, the millpond has not yet been constructed.

Quincy's Chinatown was first located at the site of the present-day Quincy High School, hence the name "China Rock" that was bestowed to that granite outcrop. Around 1900 Chinatown was "cleaned out" by local businessmen who forced the residents to move about half a mile southeast to what are now Claremont Village and the Harlem Club.

The Moon Key family is shown in their up-to-date buggy on the Meadow Valley Road west of the Plumas House Hotel. Although not much is known of this family, the 1910 census indicates Moon Key was working as a cook for the Western Pacific Railroad.

The Thompson Ranch on La Porte Road was one of American Valley's showplaces and much of it was due to the efforts of the Chinese gardener employed there. Besides raising a plethora of flowers, shrubs, and vegetables, experiments were conducted in raising silkworms on mulberry trees and growing smoking tobacco.

Until 1937 and the completion of the Feather River Highway, the only road into Quincy from the Sacramento Valley was the Oroville-Quincy Road. In this photograph the horses pulling the sleigh are wearing special horse snowshoes.

Before the advent of asphalt, mud was one of the main obstructions to smooth flowing traffic. Here, the Quincy-Greenville Stage is mired down near Blackhawk Creek on April 16, 1907.

The Plumas House Livery Stable was the number one hostelry in Quincy for 30 years. Built in 1875, this 40-foot by 80-foot brick building suffered a fire in 1911 that took off the roof. The roof was rebuilt and a new façade constructed. Note the advertisement for a minstrel show on the fence. This photograph was taken about 1877.

This *c.* 1940 view of the corner of Crescent and Main Streets shows the remodeled Plumas House Livery Stable as Hamblin's Plumas Garage. A Shell gas station has been appended to the west side.

Tom Neal's Nevada Livery Stable stood on the Meadow Valley Road about where Downtown Trailer Park is now, opposite Buchanan Street. At left is Dad Garret with Millie, his dog; "Black Dick," Mrs. Carter's horse of Crescent Mills, later Barney Schneider's horse; then Tom Neal and his daughter Della in the buggy.

The Quincy-Western Railway was the first real modern mode of transportation into Quincy from the outside world. Completed in 1910 to connect to the Western Pacific at Quincy Junction, it served the community for over 50 years. Shown here at the depot are the Grand Central Hotel and Plumas House Hotel buses.

Three types of transportation are present in this *c.* 1920 scene on Main Street. At left is Dr. Styan's home and office, followed by the Plumas County Bank before the 1929 addition, and rock-faced Clinch Building that features real gold in some of the quartz. Surveyor A.J. Watson had his offices upstairs while J.H. Reynolds ran a grocery below.

Freight wagons were still used to haul supplies into and out of Quincy in the early 1900s. Here is shown a wagon hauling a load of goods from McIntosh's Hardware Store. The top part of a kitchen stove is on top of the load, and the stovepipe is next to the driver.

Local entertainers needed a way to get around the county, and in 1918 this was their mode of travel. The Sierra Syncopaters entertained dancers for several years throughout Plumas County. George Stephan is shown with their car in front of the old Quincy Drug.

This aerial photograph taken at 10 a.m. on April 22, 1933, shows Quincy's first airport (right center with inverted "T"). Bellamy Tract now occupies this land. To the right of the airport is the Quincy Electric Light & Power Plant, and further to the right is the old Gansner Ranch.

"Sunny" Jim Rolph, governor of California, visited Quincy for the opening of the Rotary Club on May 23, 1931. His plane landed at Quincy's first airport, located on the site of today's Bellamy Tract. From left to right are Harley Flournoy, Carl Hankel, Bill Sprague, Bill Frick, Governor Rolph, Frosty Young, Bill Miller, Charlie Kerr, Owen Morris, unidentified, unidentified, and Leon Clough.

With the completion of the Feather River Highway in 1937 came bus service also. This c. 1950 photograph shows a Greyhound Lines bus bound for San Francisco in front of the Quincy Drug Store.

Four

BUILDING HOMES AND FAMILIES

The American Ranch Hotel was one of the first public houses in American Valley. It also housed the first county courthouse in a lean-to off the back of the building until 1859. It was located opposite today's Plumas Bank on the north side of Main Street.

This January 1866 view shows the old Walker Home on the corner of Court and Jackson Streets as seen from the under-construction Coburn House Hotel. In back can be seen the gabled end of Judge Goodwin's home, the first brick house in Quincy. Court Street was originally named Washington Street, but that was changed with construction of the courthouse. The men leaning on the courthouse fence were simply identified as "loafers."

In the fall of 1893 the Cate family gathered for a photograph at their pioneer ranch home near Quincy Junction. Daniel Cate was one of the valley's first settlers, built the first gristmill, and was elected first county treasurer. From left to right are (front row) Daniel Rogers Cate Sr., Hannah Loring Cate, William Jarvis, Alice Cate Jarvis, Edyth Jarvis, and Clarence Jarvis; (standing) Daniel Rogers Cate Jr., Lafayette Cate, Harry Cate, and William Jarvis.

William Alford established one of the earliest ranches and sawmills in the American Valley in the early 1850s in what is now East Quincy. Successful gold miner Samuel Lee later acquired the property and it has remained in his family ever since. Pictured in front of the house are, from left to right, Harry Lee, Cora Lee, Samuel Lee, Walter J. Ford, his daughter Ray Ford, and his wife, Annie Ford.

James Yeates and family came over Beckwourth Pass in 1851 and settled in American Valley. In 1862 they acquired this ranch, the land of which is now occupied by the Sierra Pacific Industries lumber plant.

This c. 1885 winter scene shows Anna Lena Gansner and her sister Christine on snowshoes (skis) in front of their home and the sawmill of their father, Florian Gansner. At left a man can be seen shoveling snow from the sawmill roof. The barns and other structures pictured behind the home stood until the late 1970s. The home, although greatly altered, still stands a mile west of Quincy on the Meadow Valley Road opposite the Bellamy Tract intersection.

Shown is the home of Isaac and Theresa Wheeler, said to be the first frame house built in Quincy. Water was piped into the house from a spring on the hill behind. Wheeler was in the draying and express business. Unidentified members of the Wheeler family stand on the porch in this 1860s photograph. The home stands at the east corner of Meyers Street and Meadow Valley Road.

This is the old McIntosh family home located on Meadow Valley Road just west of the county courthouse. The McIntosh family, relocated from the La Porte area, owned and operated a hardware store in Quincy. Mrs. McIntosh stands in front in the c. 1900 photograph that shows the gingerbread trim that is still intact today along the roof.

William J. Miller built this home for his wife, Carrie, and daughter Stella Fay in the 1890s. Fay was a respected teacher and music composer whose interest and endowment established the Plumas County Museum in 1964. In this c. 1905 photograph William Miller stands at left and seated on the porch are Stella Fay Miller (left) and Carrie Thompson Miller (right). The home sits on the northeast corner of Jackson and Buchanan Streets.

John D. Goodwin came to Plumas County in the 1850s, opened his law office between the Beyers' home and the present-day county museum, and was later elected the first superior court judge of Plumas County. His brick home, the first in Quincy, was built about 1863 on Jackson Street and still sits a short distance east of the Buchanan Street intersection. Judge Goodwin, shown here surrounded by his family, died in 1908.

Moving houses was a fairly common event before the advent of electric wiring and indoor plumbing. This photograph shows the Berg Home being moved into town from its original site northeast of Quincy on the Clinch Ranch in 1900. The windows have been removed and the back section detached. Its ultimate destination is the corner of Lee Way and Jackson Street where the William Watson family lived in it for over 75 years.

This house was built in 1854 by Elijah H. Pierce, later a county sheriff, just west of the present Feather Bed Bed and Breakfast. It came into the possession of Clark Lee in the latter 1860s. Lee's son later built a fine mansion-like home next to it. This 1860s photograph shows an unidentified woman at the gate.

Undeniably one of Quincy's most ornate and pretentious homes, the Clark J. Lee residence was built about 1894 on Jackson Street opposite the Court Street intersection. This stately home with all its Victorian gingerbread finery stood until it caught fire in 1969 and was razed shortly after.

Court Street gave a pleasant appearance in this 1890s view. At left is the Duncan Robertson Home, followed by Dr. Stewart's Home, then the Plumas House Hotel.

The Edward Huskinson Home was built in 1893 and is now the bed and breakfast known as the Feather Bed. The porch at left was remodeled into a Classic Revival style with upper veranda about 1915. Huskinson, brother-in-law to Barney Schneider, also owned the Quincy Drug Store, and in 1900 purchased the Cohn buildings (now Forest Office, Rebco, and Capitol Club), which has since been known as the "Huskinson Block."

James Edwards, then George Stephan, later owned this house, built *c.* 1854 by the county's first sheriff George Sharpe. It now has stone porch pillars and a foundation, both of which were added in 1918. The young boy on the porch in this *c.* 1875 photograph is unknown.

Wells Fargo agent Charles Kaulback purchased this home for his bride, Mary Loring, in 1868. About 1900 William and Amanda Beyers purchased the home. Standing on the boardwalk, from left to right, are unidentified, Mrs. Ed Garner, Mrs. Schlatter, William Beyers, and William Schlatter. The man on the left in the buggy is John Thompson, but the other is unidentified. On the veranda, the woman next to the man with the owl is Della Edwards of the Plumas House. Next door can be seen a portion of the Goodwin Law Office.

The Hall-Lawry Home located on Bradley Street was built in 1876 by Hugh S. Porter for his daughter Nellie and her new husband, Andrew "Doc" Hall. Hall moved to Quincy from Onion Valley, near La Porte, operated the Capitol Saloon, was elected county sheriff, and established the *Plumas Independent* newspaper, which ran from 1892 to 1945. The home, now owned by Plumas County is utilized by the county museum.

This bungalow-style home sat at the corner of Jackson and Coburn Streets, a site now occupied by the Plumas County Museum. Owned by C.D. Hazzard, a "capitalist" and hydraulic mine owner, the house was burned in 1966 to make room for the museum. The ladies and children in this *c.* 1905 photograph are unidentified.

W.W. Kellogg purchased this house, built in the 1860s by merchant A.P. Moore, about 1870 and lived there with his wife, Sadie, and son Boise.

The F.B. Whiting Home on the corner of Jackson and Harbison Streets was a local landmark until it burned in 1973. Fenton Whiting came to Plumas County in the early 1850s and began a dog sled express business, among other endeavors. Shown in front are members of the Whiting family in this 1890 photograph.

The intersection of Harbison and Jackson Streets was a playground for these children with their buggy wheel hoop in this c. 1885 photograph. The Fenton Whiting residence, which burned in 1973, is at right.

The B. Schneider home on the northeast corner of Jackson and Harbison Streets was built about 1903 for successful Quincy Drug Store owner Bernard "Barney" Schneider and his wife, Abbie. Barney, a Meadow Valley native, not only owned the drug store for over 20 years, he was also instrumental in electrifying Quincy in 1901.

The James Lowell Home sits at the northwest corner of Fillmore and Jackson Streets. Built in the 1870s, it sports an unusual diagonally-placed front entrance. Mettie Lowell married Judge Greenleaf G. Clough who lived across Fillmore Street from this house. Both houses remained in the same families for over 50 years. This photograph taken about 1890 shows, from left to right, James Lowell, Mettie Lowell Clough, Mrs. Lowell, and three unidentified young people.

A law partner of W.W. Kellogg, Greenleaf Greeley Clough bought this house at the northeast corner of Jackson and Fillmore Streets in 1879. He married Mettie Lowell whose parents lived across the street. Clough served as justice and superior court judge and later became an assemblyman. Remaining in his family for over 50 years, this was later the home of Sheriff Arch Braden for many years. It has since been converted to business offices.

A c. 1903 southeast view of the intersection of Jackson and Coburn Streets shows the B. Schneider home at left, then the F.B. Whiting home. At center is the John Loring home, built in 1882. At the extreme right is the Hazzard home, then the 1878 Variel home, followed by the home

This 1908 wintertime view shows the intersection of Jackson and Harbison Streets. At left is part of the business district; at center is the 1855 Masonic Hall, then the Schneider home, the

of H.P. Wormley (now Van Gilder) and then the present Trumbo family home. The last house is now the site of the Steiner home. Note the open field and apple orchard right of center, now covered with homes.

1902 Berg home, the 1870s Lowell home, and at extreme right, the 1860s Whiting home.

The Gus and Anna Berg home is shown here during the winter of 1911. This Queen Anne–style home was built in 1902.

A.W. Keddie takes time from his busy surveying schedule to pose with his wife, Margaret (left); son Walter; and daughters Margaret and Helen in this c. 1880 view. The home was razed in the 1950s to build the house now occupying the site. Keddie produced an immense amount of work, including four outstanding county maps between 1866 and 1912, and lived to the age of 82.

Shown in this 1908 photograph are, from left to right, Lyle (Hank) Dedmon, Frank Dedmon, and Jim Maxwell. The little girl is Echo Dedmon. The Dedmons were practical gold miners and freighters, and in later years, Frank Dedmon, known as "Shorty," married Florence Campbell, a big supporter of the Plumas County Museum. The house sits on Jackson Street opposite the Plumas Unified School District offices.

This uniquely adorned Victorian home was built between East and Roche Streets by Benjamin L. "Bonanza" Jones for his wife, Annie. "Bonanza" earned his nickname from a $75,000 pocket of gold he found in the Johnsville region. Annie is sitting on the porch while Ben stands by the railing.

Judge Edmund T. Hogan built this home sometime around 1860 for his family. Hogan, an early pioneer, was also newspaper editor of the *Fillmore Banner* during the 1850s. His descendants included Ida "Billie" Hogan Gronvold, who was county recorder for many years. The house, shown *c.* 1890, sits on High Street opposite the Fillmore Street intersection.

This interestingly shaped house is the John Barker home, situated on the southwest side of Quincy between present-day West High Street and Monte Vista Avenue. Pictured, from left to right, are John Barker, an unidentified dog, Maria E. Barker, and Nellie Barker Erwin. This photograph was taken about 1895. The R.L. Erwin family later purchased the property.

Joshua Variel, a carpenter, built this home in 1878. In 1896 he sold it to Sheriff John Bransford, who then sold it to Louis Peter (shown here with his family). After Peter died in the house in 1916 it was remodeled, then went through a succession of owners. In 1989 it came into the possession of the Plumas County Museum and was meticulously restored to its 1890s appearance.

The Whitlock home, built about 1877, was originally situated on the northeast corner of Church and Main Streets. Maj. James H. Whitlock, who lived there until 1903, came to Plumas County in 1850 and served as county treasurer and as a state legislator. Harley C. Flournoy bought the home about 1908 and had it moved to its present site about half a block west on Main Street. From left to right are unidentified, Robbie Whitlock, Ethel Whitlock, Mrs. Whitlock, and J.H. Whitlock.

In 1911, travelers passing by the Clinch Ranch, situated at the Lee Road and Quincy Junction Road intersection, saw this Sears and Roebuck catalog home under construction. It cost $1,995 delivered.

It is unknown who built this home, only that it was around 1900 or before. About 1956 it was converted into the Lutheran Church at its location on High Street opposite the Methodist Fellowship Hall.

Five

PUBLIC SERVICES
AND FACILITIES

This 1866 view of the Plumas County Courthouse was taken from the Coburn House Hotel site. The hotel had burned in 1865 and was under reconstruction. When sign maker Jackie Kinsey was asked why he put the oval hole in the Coburn House sign, he replied that "I had one laying around the shop, and thought I'd use it."

The hall of records was built adjacent to the courthouse in 1895. In this 1910 photograph are pictured, from left to right, (front row) Plumas C. Clough, assistant recorder; J.F. Spooner, treasurer; and Horace McBeth, clerk and auditor; (back row) Mr. Anderson, public accountant; Louis P. Mori, tax collector; and Leon L. Clough, recorder.

In this c. 1918 photograph the county courthouse, hall of records, and jail are seen for the last time together before construction began on the new courthouse.

This view from the Capitol Saloon's second floor shows the courthouse grounds after the original building was moved to the east to accommodate the construction of the new one. Cement forms are beginning to rise around the hall of records. At center is the brick jail and to its left is the washhouse and woodshed. The latter was moved to Lawrence Street next to the Catholic church by R.D. Tucker.

Dedication of the cornerstone for the new courthouse by the Masons took place on September 11, 1919, with a huge celebration following. At left is the old courthouse, the forms for the first floor of the new courthouse, and at the extreme right, the hall of records.

This close-up view shows the old courthouse minus one of its porch columns tucked in behind the east wing of the new courthouse. Efforts to donate the aged structure to a religious or civic group failed and it was demolished shortly after completion of the new courthouse in 1921.

Dedication of the new county courthouse took place on California Statehood Admission Day, September 9, 1921. Bunting and flags bedecked the new structure while crowds partook of food and beverages. The governor of California made a speech and local bands provided music.

Until 1854 Quincy had no school. The first in the area was at Elizabethtown, though there was no building. In 1857, through donations of lumber and labor, the residents of Pioneer District, now East Quincy, constructed the first school building in the county. In 1974 the Pioneer School was moved to its present site at the Plumas County Fairgrounds.

G.W. Meylert built the Quincy Grammar School in 1876 at a cost of $4,000. Vertical timbers were added to reinforce the brick walls, which were found to be unstable. Nonetheless it continued to be used until the 1905 school replaced it.

This photograph of the Quincy Elementary School student body was taken shortly after the school was finished in 1905. It replaced the 1876 brick school, which was failing structurally. A wing was added to the right side of the school in 1918. The last classes were held in 1951 and today it serves as the Plumas Unified School District offices.

In 1911 a temporary high school was erected on the site of the old Chinatown at China Rock. It housed students until the permanent school was finished in 1914.

The Quincy High School building was the pride of Quincy when it was completed in 1914. Built as the Plumas County High School, it later became Quincy High when the county's other communities built their own schools. The last graduating class from this building was in 1973. This imposing brick structure was demolished in the late 1970s to make room for a parking lot.

The county hospital originally sat on Beskeen Lane where the county cemetery is located. In 1915 a new hospital was constructed 1.5 miles north of Quincy where the County Annex is now located. This structure was demolished in the late 1950s and a new hospital built.

R.D. "Tune" Haun is shown hauling a load of pumpkins raised at the old County Hospital by Len Remick around 1915. In the back can be seen the maintenance shed and the morgue.

The Quincy Cemetery at the turn of the century presents a rather stark appearance compared to today. In the center is the tombstone of William Wagner, longtime owner of Buck's Ranch, now Bucks Lake. The small oaks have grown to stately trees over the past 100 years.

Quincy's first water works were installed in 1878 when Judge Goodwin brought pipes into town from a reservoir in Goodwin Ravine. Fire hydrants were installed on some of the street corners, and it was said the stream from a fire hose reached as high as the top of the flagpole on the old courthouse. In this October 1911 photograph Miss Mattie Goodwin, the owner, is accompanied by Heine Hoffman at the reservoir.

Quincy Hose Company No. 1 assembled for this July 4, 1879 photograph on the north side of Quincy's Main Street. From left to right are W.W. Kellogg, unidentified, J.M. Chapman, Ed Garner, B.B. Hughes, Wm. Ward, A.W. Keddie, George Wilson, Marcus Light, William Goodwin, G.B. Sumner, W.H. Lake, "Doc" Hall, R.W. Gill, John Smith, Al Wilson, C.M. Blakesley, R.H.F. Variel, Fenton B. Whiting, Ed Huskinson, and Dan Cate.

The Quincy Fire Department chiefs posed for this 1868 photograph. From left to right are J.H. Ayers, Henry Meisser, and William Shinn. The museum has one of the speaking trumpets the men are holding in its collection.

Around 1894 the Quincy Fire Department moved to the south side of Main Street. Shown here is their new building where Great Northern now stands.

The Quincy Volunteer Fire Department is shown in the same building on Main Street in 1934. From left to right are (front row) Mel Schooler, Bill Barrett, and Johnny Redstreake; (back row) Bill Hamblin, Bill Hardgrave, Doug Redstreake, Bob Young, Leo Kelsey, Larry Hardgrave, Marion Kelsey, Wendel Hogan, Plumie Stokes, Elton Brown, and Bob Wilson.

In early 1946 the Quincy Volunteer Fire Department turned out for a photograph at their new Lawrence Street station. From left to right are Ernie Ward, Elwin Whipple, Glen Dursteller, J.C. Ferguson, Bus Egbert, Eddie Dursteller (Chief), Earl "Silvertip" Bowen, Jack Donnenwirth, Chris Egbert, Jack McQuarrie, Kenny Thomas, Paul Vaughn, Mike Gabor, Charlie Hannah, Johnny Redstreake, and Don Alexander.

The Plumas County Fair has been in continuous operation since 1859 and at the county fairgrounds in Quincy since 1946. This c. 1960 aerial view of the fairgrounds looks north.

Six

LEISURE TIME, ACTIVITIES, AND EVENTS

The International Order of Odd Fellows (IOOF) was an important fraternal organization in 19th-century America. Here they are shown having a parade along with the Quincy Brass Band on Friday, April 26, 1895.

A canopy was erected in front and along the east side of the courthouse to shade the long tables loaded with sandwiches and drinks for the participants of the July 4, 1896 celebration. All kinds of athletic exercises were scheduled, including bicycle races for men and ladies, a "fat man" race for those over 200 pounds, foot races, egg races, wheelbarrow races, sack races, jumps, vaults, shot putting, hammer throwing, and greased-pole climbing. A real highlight was the greased pig chase!

The Goddess of Liberty (center, Nellie Chandler Gansner) is surrounded by some of our nation's states for Quincy's July 4, 1896 celebration. From left to right are Maude White Welden, Jennie Sutton, Annie Otis, Margaret Hogan, Ethel Fletcher, Birdie Haun, Pearl Whiting Clinch, Cecilia Hogan Chamberlain, Zetta Blakesley Clark, Maggie Parks of Oroville, Amy Sauer Stampfli, and Annie Sutton Diceley.

Parades were a favorite for Quincy residents, particularly on July 4, 1896. This buggy is on Jackson Street in front of the Clough home. In the rear can be seen the Lowell family home. The little boy standing in back is unidentified, but next is Mattie Clough, Harry Wormley, and Frank Robertson as the driver.

The July 4, 1896 parade, shown here, was headed by the Quincy Brass Band and included five or more floats containing the Goddess of Liberty and representatives of the different states and California. It assembled at 9 a.m. in front of Courthouse Square and was to march at 9:30, sharp!

Besides the July 4, 1896 bicycle race shown here, a spirited footrace also provided physical diversion from eating and drinking for Quincy's aspiring athletes.

R.D. "Tune" Haun (left) and Charlie Emerson pit their fighting cocks at Quincy in this photograph taken in the late 1890s. The Hauns raised gamecocks for sale to the Virginia City miners of Nevada during the 1860s and 1870s. This once popular but bloody sport was finally stopped in the early 1900s.

The Quincy baseball team is shown here on September 29, 1906. From left to right are (front row) Arch Braden, Herbert Hail, Dick Chamberlain, Bob Hall, and Harry Goodwin; (back row) Dr. Stewart, John Wilson, Warren Braden, Will Clinch, Frank Smith, Lafayette Cate, and U.S. Webb.

The Quincy Colts lined up to show off their new uniforms on July 15, 1906. From left to right are (front row) Sam Leavitt (holding a hoe) and Plumas Morton (first base); (middle row) Art Berg, Frank Robertson, Ernest Watson, and Harry Wormley (pitcher); (back row) Jake Stephan, "Boots" Thomas (catcher), Bob Fletcher, and Harry Hume.

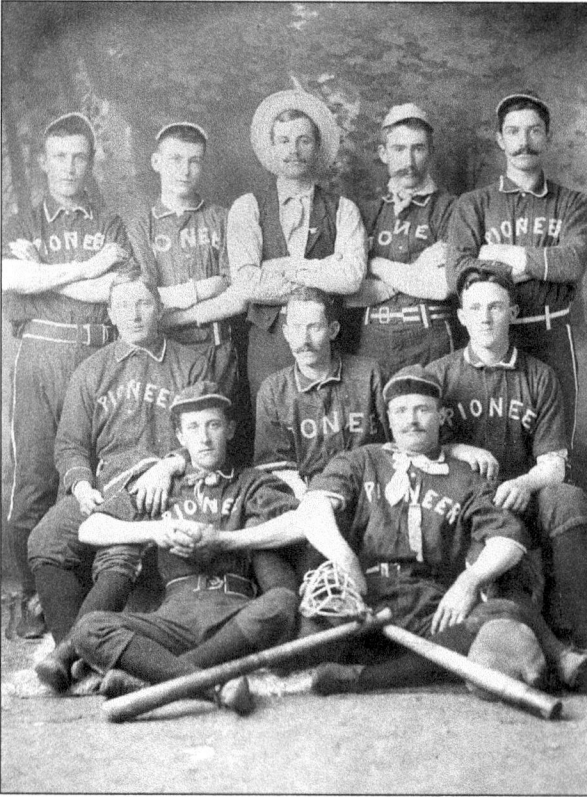

The year 1906 was a banner one for baseball in Quincy. Shown here are Pioneer team members, from left to right: (front row) Dan Finlayson and Will Clinch; (middle row) Fayette Cate, Van Parks, and Dan Robertson; (back row) John Finlayson, Leonard Hail, Frank Smith, Warren Braden, and Harry Cate.

This gathering of men and boys are hanging around the porch of the Plumas House to receive news via telegraph of the Gans-Nelson fight in Goldfield, Nevada, on Monday, September 3, 1906.

The Quincy Brass Band marches and plays in honor of the first passenger train over the Western Pacific Railroad on August 22, 1910. Behind them are the Grand Central Hotel, the Sportsman Saloon, and Dorsch's Hardware.

When the weather was cold enough ice skating was a popular sport in Quincy. This 1910 group of enthusiasts are on a small pond just south of present-day Gansner Airfield.

"The Spirit of Spring Pageant of the Wildflowers," held on June 7, 1928, was a huge success. The entire town of Quincy turned out for the event, which was held on the courthouse plaza. Spectators filled the plaza, adorned the courthouse windowsills, and even watched from the tops of the business houses across the street. Comprised of almost all of the town's school-age children, the event boasted unique costumes created by their mothers.

Shown here, from left to right, are "The Fairies": (front row) Leah ?, Beverly Bar, Beth Moncur, Alma Jean Hogan, Theda Ball, and Melba Ayoob; (back row) Nannette Bar, Mary Hall, Ruth Dunn, Evelyn Pauly, Meera Remick, Zola Tucker, and Bessie Que.

Even the boys were forced into the Wildflower program, and those in this group were called "The Heralds." From left to right, they are unidentified, Fred Wolfe, Carlton Droege, Elwood Hunt, and Ralph "Buddy" Kerr.

This group of children gathered as "The Bingo Express" in 1914 for a parade. They are pictured by the gazebo on the east side lawn of the courthouse and are, from left to right (front row) unidentified, William Clinch, Wayne Braden, unidentified, Rae Strickland, Gwendolyn Moseley, unidentified, Orvall Myers, unidentified, Jessie McSween, Thelma Short, Beryl Schroeder, Ray Mullen, and Anita Bolton. On the donkey is Donna Sprague, and in the buggy are ? Aldrich, Helen Short, three unidentified children, Tennye Flournoy, Nola Case, and three more unidentified children.

The 1930s saw a resurgence of interest in gold rush-era history. These fellows are "hanging" a desperado in front of the county courthouse.

This group of local young ladies climbed aboard the old Plumas House Bus, a horse-drawn wagon, in preparation for a parade in the 1930s. From left to right are Doris "Sis" Tucker, Jean Harris, Jessie Finch, Mary Ethel Hogan, Zola Tucker, Janet Cotter, Connie Small, unidentified, Nedra Bordwell, and Barbara Baldwin.

The winter of 1889–1890 saw a significant amount of snow. If it weren't for his black dots, this Dalmatian would be lost in the snow. This westward view also shows George Kuhn's Shoe Shop at the extreme left.

Christmas Eve 1893 was a high water event. This view from the porch of the Plumas House looks north across the American Valley. Directly in front is the Dew Drop Inn and running through the center is the main road out of town.

This March 20, 1907 view looks north down Meyers Street and shows the damage one little seasonal creek can do when it gets large enough. On the left is the Roy Garland residence, and on the right is the Wheeler home.

Snowstorms occur every year in Quincy, but some are a little bigger than others. This January 16, 1911 storm was touted as bringing in 7.5 feet on the level, though it was later conceded that the claim was a bit of an exaggeration. The men's heads poke up in front of the Huskinson Block in downtown Quincy.

This March 1937 scene shows Main Street as viewed to the west. Kilpatrick's Grocery is first on the right, followed by Goon Moon's Shell Station, then Nebel's Garage. The huge snow bank separated eastbound and westbound traffic.

December 1937 was one of the wetter months on record. This view from a rooftop on Railway Avenue looks west across the valley. Railroad cars at right are left stranded while water almost reaches the tops of the fence posts along the main highway.

This conveyor-type machine was used to remove snow from Main Street by the road department in the 1930s and 1940s.

WINTER of '52
Quincy Calif

The "Winter of '52" is still remembered by many as one of the biggest snowstorms to hit Quincy in decades. Eight feet of snow piled up between January 12 and 14 amid gale force winds. This view of Main Street a few days later looks east and shows business as usual.

Seven

PEOPLE

Flora Gansner is shown in stylish riding habit on her horse in Quincy. Born in 1868, she was one of eight children belonging to Christina and Florian Gansner, a successful sawmill owner west of Quincy. Flora married Harley C. Flournoy in 1886. He served as county clerk, auditor, and assessor over the years, and was one of the founders of Plumas County Bank in 1903. Flora died in 1941.

This early 1880s photograph shows some of the movers and shakers of Quincy and Plumas County. From left to right are (front row) F.B. Hosselkus, U.S. Webb, and Ed Huskinson; (back row) Dan Cate, Will Edwards, and John Sutton.

This c. 1890 formal photograph of Judge Clough and family includes, from left to right, Leon Clough, Mettie Clough (who died at age 17), Judge G.G. Clough, Ruth Clough, and Mrs. Mettie Lowell Clough.

This is the extended family of rancher John W. Thompson, *c.* 1895. Pictured, from left to right, are (front row) Mrs. Thompson, Stella Fay Miller, and John Thompson; (back row) Dodie Thompson, William J. Miller, Carrie Thompson Miller, and John Thompson Jr.

These children gathered together for some summertime fun just north of Quincy on the Robertson Ranch, now the Philip Bresciani Ranch, about 1909. Pictured, from left to right, are (front row) Martha Spooner, Frances Mayfield, Zola Semans, Nellie Robinson, Maude Strickland, and Junior Robertson; (middle row) Eliz Robinson, Margaret Ball, and Velma Semans; (back row) William Robinson, Charles Fletcher, George Robinson, and Horace Bull.

Local businessmen Ed Garner, Jacob Stephan, and Edward Northope enjoy a quiet cigar inside what is believed to be the Plumas House in this 1890 photograph.

This 1895 photograph, titled "Escaped from State Penitentiary $100 Reward Each," shows, from left to right (front row) Will Lamkin, John Thompson, Gus Mann, H.C. Flournoy, unidentified, and Tune Haun; (middle row) J.V. Parks, Harry Cate, Jack McKeowen, Fred Smith, W.J. Clinch, Dan Finlayson, Dan Robertson, W.J. Miller, Fred Kaulback, and Morgan Haun; (back row) John Finlayson, Leigh Dunning, Frank Smith, Fayette Cate, Ferd Hogan, unidentified, Fred Gansner, and Warren Braden.

The Quincy Brass Band is pictured on the lawn of the Plumas House about 1875. From left to right are (front row) Charlie Barker, John Porter, Will Graham, Davis Hall, George Wilson, Watt Bell, and Jackie Kinsey; (back row) Dick Bell, Clark Lee, John Barker, Charlie Larison, Steve Kinsey, Will Edwards, George Engleback, Ben Gansner, Jud Coburn, Hugh Porter, and Jack Clinch.

This photograph of the Quincy Brass Band was taken when they were between uniforms. Dated 1881, but thought to be somewhat later, it shows, from left to right, George Wilson, John Porter, Walter "Watt" Bell, unidentified, George Fletcher, Dan Finlayson, John Thompson, George Engleback, Lee Erwin, Warren Braden, Will Clinch, Will Lamkin, John Barker, and John "Jack" Clinch.

In 1900 the Quincy Brass Band was sporting all new uniforms and instruments. Pictured here are, from left to right, (front row) Arthur C. Berg, George Wilson (director), John E. Wilson, and J.O. Moncur; (second row) Jack McKeowen, Morgan Haun, Ralph Lake, Charles S. Meyers, Henry J. Hoffman, Pat McHager, and Harold Meyers; (third row) Horace McBeth, Wiley Forson, Mills Fletcher, Barrett Huskinson, Joe Little, and Charles Kerr; (back row) Fayette Cate, Leon Clough, Harry Cate, William Clinch, Will Light, Dr. B.J. Lasswell, and Warren Braden.

On October 13, 1899, Quincy turned out to welcome its heroes home from the Spanish-American War. Pictured in front of the Huskinson home are, from left to right, Fred Smith of Quincy, Jack McLaughlin of La Porte, and Frank Smith of Butterfly Valley.

This c. 1900 photograph shows Mrs. Tucker's art class in an outdoor session. From left to right are the instructor Mrs. Tucker, Cathie Mills, Bertha Fouche Wormley, Mamie Cate, Mattie Goodwin, Della Edwards, and Carrie Thompson Miller. Mrs. Miller produced a number of excellent watercolors now in the museum's collection.

Barrett Huskinson is shown with his new bicycle in front of his home on Jackson Street around 1900. He later ran a pharmacy in Roseville, California, as well as being the owner of the Quincy Drug Store, a business his father, Ed Huskinson, had also once owned.

March of 1890 found Mr. Yager and Mr. Miller leading this sleigh with Mr. Massey and Mr. Konradi as wheelers. An ailing Mrs. Jane Edwards is the passenger with Mr. Byers bringing up the rear in downtown Quincy.

This new-fangled talking machine brought Harley C. Flournoy, Flora Gansner Flournoy, Barney Schneider, and Abbie Huskinson Schneider together at the Schneider home to hear the latest in hit tunes in 1907.

These pack mules are waiting in front of the Ford & Lee Store around 1900 for supplies to haul back to a local mine. The one on the right is patiently allowing one of the Fletcher family children to sit on him.

The Masons have been one of the most enduring fraternal organizations in Plumas County, with the Plumas Lodge being established in 1854. This group of Masons posed for a late 1950s photograph. From left to right are (front row) J.O. Moncur, Leon Clough, Len Thayer, Solon Luzzader, and unidentified; (back row) Lee Larison, George O'Kelly, Freeman Grover, Joe Crivello, Orvall Meyers, Vaughn Edwards, Bill Bailey (in light jacket), Clay Elworthy, Bruce Myers, Bert Dale, Bill Slaten, and Guy Coykendall.

These folks are duded up for the county fair in the late 1940s. From left to right are Lois Turley, Sam Eckstein, Mabel Mulleague, Mildred Saap, and Barney Eckstein, standing in front of Quincy Mercantile, now Great Northern.

Chris Egbert provides oil to the "misery whip" being manned by an unidentified logging championship participant at the county fair during the mid-1950s. Behind him in the tin hat is Link Peckinpah, the county chamber manager.

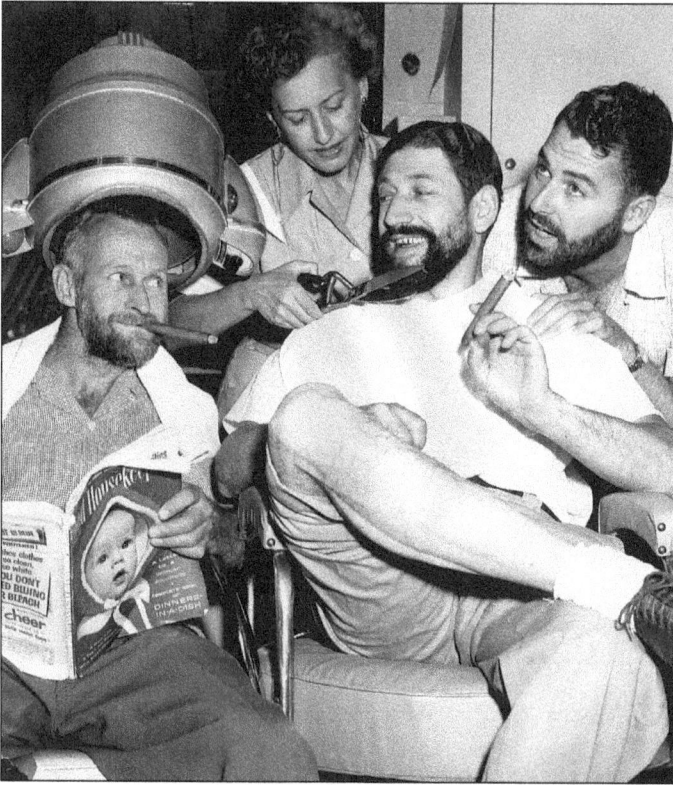

These "Whiskerinos" are really hamming it up for the camera. Local men grew beards during the fair as a promotional gimmick. Seen here in the early 1950s getting "beautified" are, from left to right, Douglas Redstreake, Joe Crivello, and "Tex" Owens. Georgia Cokor is wielding the shears.

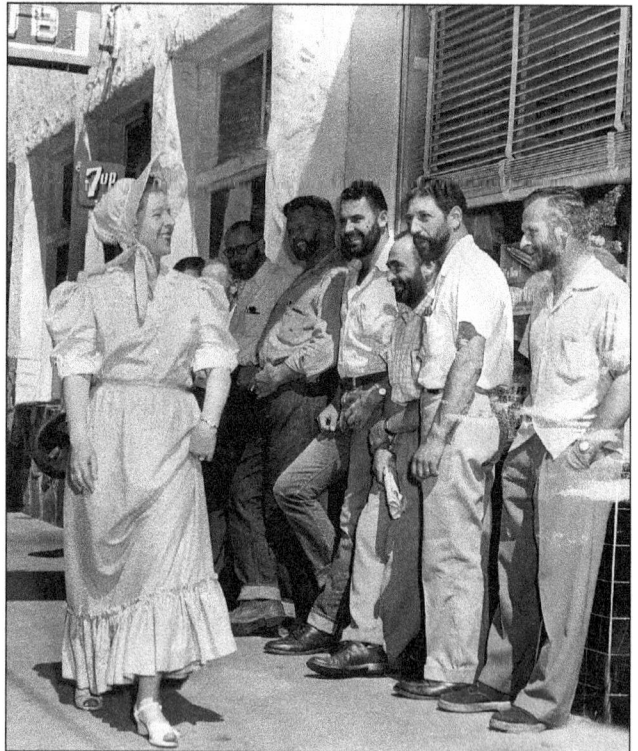

"Whiskerinos" have lined up in front of the Grand Club on Main Street in the early 1950s to ogle and whistle at passing ladies. From left to right are Ernie Chaney, Kermit Fuller, Tex Owens, John Ayoob, Joe Crivello, and Douglas Redstreake. The passing lady is Jewel Frierdich.

114

The Plumas County High School band poses on China Rock in 1930. From left to right are (front row) George Chaffey, four unidentified, Beulah Larison, and Harlene Chaffey; (second row) Gayle Rodgers, Muriel Smith, Margaret Young, Douglas Redstreake, five unidentified, Bud Young, and Beth Moncur; (third row) Margaret Chaffey, Margaret Fair, and the rest are unidentified except for Mr. Riley in the dark jacket.

The Junior Chamber of Commerce is shown here in the late 1950s. From left to right are (front row) Chet Johnson and Ray Edmundson; (middle row) Bob Myers, Vadney Murray, Stanley Young, unidentified, Bob Dellinger, and Jennings Van Fossen; (back row) Dennis Geil, Frank Jenks, Boyd Tieslau, Jerry Pellet, Jim Gossett, and Don Price.

E Clampus Vitus, or "Clampers," is a fraternal organization formed during the California Gold Rush years. Since then it died out and was revived several times in Plumas County, the latest era beginning in 1952. Shown dedicating Rich Bar in 1957, from left to right, are Bruce McDonald (with the Hewgag), unidentified, Bob Erbeck, unidentified, L.V. "Duke" Aaserude, unidentified, and Clarence Schott.

Outlandish antics are a hallmark of Clampers. This 1959 parade is composed, from left to right, as follows: Frank Gasper, Bud Grover, unidentified Poor Blind Candidate, unidentified, S.L. Bailey, goat, Kermit Fuller, and Jack Atthowe. The age-old question, "Is Clampers a historical drinking group, or a drinking historical group?" ensures the continuation of the fraternity as long as enough remain to debate it.

The 20-30 Club in the late 1950s was comprised of these young fellows. From left to right are (front row) Jim Finnegan, Paul Whipple, Dick Dessa, and Con Turner; (back row) Jim Gossett and unidentified.

The Native Daughters of the Golden West were a major factor in documenting and preserving Quincy and Plumas County's past. Pictured here, from left to right, are Lena Droege, Florence Jacks, Mary Leavitt, and Kathryn Pauly at the Bucks Ranch dedication in 1931.

Cecil Koenig holds up a jug before a presentation on collecting old bottles held at a fledgling Plumas County Historical Society meeting at the Sloat Town Hall around 1963. Margaret Mason shuts her eyes as if afraid Koenig will drop it.

This Rebecca Installation featured the following ladies, from left to right: (front row) Bea Howlett, Grace Buus, Mary Dunn, Claire Schultz, Myrtte McCoy, Lucy Prestidge, and Alice Taylor; (middle row) Janie Hogan, Betty Hilton, Alice Bashford, Meta Erbeck, Alva Wakeman, Joyce Herndon, and Beatrice Hunt; (back row) Ruth Reid, Louise Robinson, Annie Johnson, Frances Bishop, Dorothy Chapman, Marge Burch, Ruth Myers, and Sara Blankenship.

Eight

AMERICAN VALLEY AND QUINCY OVER TIME

The mid-1870s saw a building boom in Quincy. This was due in large part to the success of the area's hydraulic gold mines. In this *c.* 1876 view looking east most of Quincy's important public buildings as well as many early homes are visible. The road in the foreground is the Meadow Valley Road and the low saddle in the hills in back is Cemetery Hill.

When this view was taken about 1890 from behind Quincy looking north, only a few buildings are visible. The Stinson Ranch is at the extreme left, where the Long Bridge crossed Spanish Creek. A few buildings are tucked in along what is now Beskeen Lane, and the White Ranch is just a speck far across the valley.

This 1890s view is of American Valley to the west. To the right of center is the Long Bridge across Spanish Creek. Note the thick riparian growth where the Gansner Airport is now located.

This c. 1910 view of Quincy shows snow-capped Claremont Peak in the background. Gansner's Slough winds lazily across the valley, and in the bottom right, amidst the pines, can be seen one of Quincy's two "Red Light" houses. These houses of prostitution were later moved into Quincy as residences.

When this photograph was taken in 1932 Moon's Auto Court was well established (left of center), but the block between Railway Avenue and Fillmore Street on the north side of Main was empty except for Goon Moon's gas station. The large barns in the foreground and the open area in the upper left have all been replaced with housing. The hillside in back had been logged using horses and log chutes in 1925 in an effort to preserve the beauty of the town's backdrop.

The little hamlet of Quincy presents a sleepy appearance in this 1890 view from China Rock looking to the west. To the left of center is the 1876 brick school, and to the left of that is the Methodist Church.

This *c.* 1928 photograph shows the Quincy Lumber Company railroad tracks crossing the main road into Quincy at the Quincy Junction Road intersection. The path along the road was used by students to walk to the high school, the spot this photograph was taken from.

This c. 1900 view of Quincy looks northwest from behind town. In the foreground is the Methodist Church and to its right is the first brick school.

Note the changes in this 1910 view of Quincy from the same spot. The 1905 school has replaced the brick one, the Quincy railroad is present, and a number of houses have popped up in the foreground.

This April 13, 1907 view of American Valley and Quincy shows some of the remaining floodwaters of March still in the valley. Visible at the base of Radio Hill is China Rock, now occupied by the high school.

This 1950s aerial view of American Valley was taken looking west. The at left area now occupied by East Quincy is heavily wooded, while Radio Hill has been denuded by fire. Lee Road breaks away to the right from the 1942–1944 alignment of Highway 70. Stacks of drying lumber can be seen at the Meadow Valley Mill to the right of Lee Road.

This shot of Quincy is to the west from Radio Hill showing the extent of the town about 1906. Note that the sawmill is absent in the foreground. Lawrence Street is but a trace bearing right off Main Street.

This view of Quincy in 1921 from behind the high school shows the Quincy mill and its drying yards but no millpond as yet.

126

In another photograph c. 1929 from the same spot as the previous photograph we can see the Quincy Lumber Company sawmill and pond in place. The mill was in operation in late 1913.

By 1953 a number of changes had occurred in Quincy. North of Lawrence Street are the U.S. Forest Service buildings constructed in 1933. The Quonset hut Rose's Market is just east of that, and the highway has been realigned left of the high school through the mill's drying yards.

This 1960s shot from the "Q" above the high school shows an open field, again where the Quincy mill once stood.

This view of Quincy taken around 1998 from about the same spot shows the shopping center where the mill once sat.

Visit us at
arcadiapublishing.com

www.ingramcontent.com/pod-product-compliance
Lightning Source LLC
Chambersburg PA
CBHW050542110426
42813CB00008B/2232